An Introduction to the Dreamtime

Australian Aboriginal mysticism explained and explored.

Contents

Introduction

The question arises: what is the Australian Aboriginal Dreamtime? The answer to this is obtained via a brief, though circuitous route.

If we, in a strictly non-gender sense, divide human capacity for perceiving reality into masculine and feminine faculties, we very soon learn that 'the real world' is not as easily grasped as we might have hoped—reality is multi-dimensional. Indeed, the masculine, external, strictly material perception proves to be of relatively minor importance. No, this is not to say that one can walk through walls and closed doors without acquiring a bloodied and probably broken nose.

One simple tool that will help us in our quest is to give each of our two faculties a symbol: 1 (One) for the masculine external and 0 (Zero) for the feminine internal. And let us also assert here that all men and all women have both masculine and feminine (1 and 0) perception capacity.

What we know of the relatively minor masculine is that it's a chatterbox and a bossy boots. From the moment we wake up till the time we go to sleep, this egotistical little dictator, made grossly insecure by the physical world's constant threats to our safety, is continuously shouting in our heads: 'mind this', 'be careful of that', 'get real', 'pay attention'. On the other hand, the feminine has long since given up trying to compete with the idiot it has to work with: after all, within the confines of its job description, One is doing as it should. A way in which we might grasp the relativity of these two is to say that where One is a bush telegraph, Zero is a cell phone with Internet capacity. For myself, I would say that Zero gives me, and anyone else for that matter, direct access to the humungous main-frame computer at the centre of the universe—God. And by 'the centre of the universe' I mean the centre of myself—or yourself.

Ancient civilizations everywhere were clearly concerned with the balancing of these two forces. It is *a)* clear that they succeeded and *b)* obvious that this did not result in lives spent in navel-gazing. Our world is strewn with clear and unambiguous evidence that Megalithic Man was a scientific genius.

An Introduction to the Dreamtime

Australian Aboriginal mysticism explained and explored.

By R Lewis

About the Author

Author R. Lewis published six books on myth and ancient religion, including *A Beginner's Guide to Australian Aboriginal Art* and *A Beginner's Guide to Australian Aboriginal Words*, and he worked in the Aboriginal Arts Industry for many years.

Author R Lewis,
Edited by Jean Argyle – jargyle@ozemail.com.au

ISBN 978 098 035 2177

This edition published in 2009 by Gecko Books
Reprinted 2012
Reprinted 2015
Reprinted in 2017
P.O. Box 118 Marleston SA 5033
Email: sales@jbbooks.com.au
Printed in China through Asia Pacific Offset

But it is in the nature of One to abhor compromise; it demands the right to dominate, that is, it thinks SNAGs are wimps. Its most recent and successful rebellion and rise to power was consolidated in the hands of René Descartes (1596-1650) and his horde of Cartesian philosophers. If, they said, you can't touch, taste, smell, hear or see it, then it just isn't there. Later, they came up with the idea of lobotomizing those hapless heretics for whom 'it' would not go away. Cartesian insanity reached its peak when shock troops were sent to countries like Australia to root out the heresy by exterminating the people who clung to it. Yes, at its base, colonialism was an offshoot of One's rise to power, a phenomenon *seeded* at the dawn of the Piscean Age.

In the West, these same heretics came to be known to us as Hermeticists, Cabbalists and Alchemists. The transmutation of lead into gold became a metaphor for balancing the hemispheres of the mind. The alchemist was his own laboratory and he, himself, was the experiment. His Eastern counterparts left us with the concept of balancing the Yin and the Yang. And they all went to their graves telling us that we should make the inner as the outer and the below like unto the above. Today's materialistic and mechanistic world, the fragmentation of religion and subsequent fragmentation of values, the fragmentation of knowledge and, ultimately, the fragmentation of the individual can all be seen as springing from the Cartesian consolidation of One's rise to power.

Its flower, of course, is the bucket of bolts we call a computer. And with this monstrosity, the Cartesians have philosophically shot themselves in the foot, for its basis is the binary system—an integration and utilisation of ones and zeros; it would seem that the below is like unto the above after all.

Yes, dear reader, the Australian Aboriginal Dreamtime is an alchemical, hermetic, Jungian type of psychological process by which balancing the one and the zero gives us a total grasp of reality. And furthermore, the Dreaming is not yesterday, today or tomorrow—it is timeless; it is now and it is forever. Through it, all mind and soul is connected; it is one.

So, dear brother and sister, read on and remember to keep the faith and keep on dreaming.

Beginning Dreaming

The sticks and horseshoes are respectively men and women, depicted here upon three islands. Very ancient tradition says the people departed the islands to the north of Australia (the Indonesian group) and crossed the Timor Sea to Australia. Recent research has indicated that they had originally lived in the Indian sub-continent but were driven out by the southerly drift of the Arya tribes.

Tradition says a boastful man threw his boomerang across the ocean and claimed it had reached the furthest island on the other side. His claim was, of course, disputed and derided. But the solution was provided by a little boy who cut out the entrails of a koala. He then proceeded to blow into them until they formed a rainbow bridge across the ocean. All the disputants crossed over the entrail bridge and, arriving in Australia, they became the mothers and fathers of the Aborigines.

Frill-necked Lizard

Walek, the frill-necked lizard, led the lizard people of Nelgi Island (fifty kilometres north of Cape York). They had yet to discover fire and their cooking procedures, using sun heated stones, were subsequently long and laborious. But Walek had a sister living in the far-off islands of Papua New Guinea from where smoke was often seen to rise. It was Walek who undertook the long and dangerous journey to his sister's village. At first, she refused him and then gave him a cold coal, but he persisted and finally returned to a hero's welcome with the gift of fire.

Because lizards are connected with thieves (stealing fire) and shape shifting, we might relate this to the little boy who came from nowhere and would never tell anyone about himself. He was very lovable and was adopted by the tribe, but soon all manner of things, except the Tjurunga and other sacred objects, began to go missing. He was eventually caught and was about to have a thrashing administered when a falling spear injured him and he died. His body was covered with bark but the next day it had disappeared. In its place, there was only a lizard.

Waterhole Dreaming

When, in the beginning Dreaming, three beautiful young women came down from the stars to visit the earth, they went walkabout. From time to time they needed to pass water; where they did so, they left sacred pools. If a mortal man should come upon one of these waterholes and drink from it, the liquid would greatly increase his capacity to learn the Dreaming knowledge.

It is this process that took men out of their primal embryonic stage, in which they lived as the Inapatua: formless and shadowy beings with only faint traces of what they would one day become. The Numbakulla were two sky-brothers who, whilst looking down upon the earth, decided to come with their knives and give final shape to these plastic creatures. They turned them into men and women and sent them off to populate Australia.

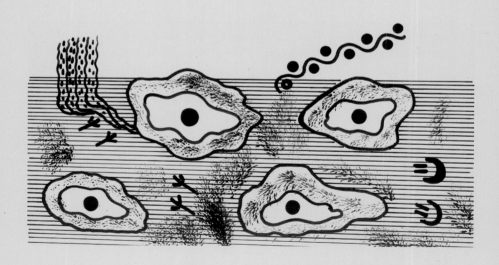

The Birth of Emu

Of the three sisters who came down from the stars of Orion's Belt, two returned and one was obliged to stay on earth and play the role of Tya (the earth spirit). Because the emu is a flightless bird, it symbolizes the third sister's being a prisoner on earth. But the emu is a dowdy, ill mannered and ill-tempered creature, not the best choice for the incarnation of the ultimate female.

The first thing Emu created was the Tnatanja Pole, it was covered in down and reached up to the stars. But she left it in the care of Termite Woman, whereupon it was given to breaking and snapping where she had eaten into it. It was this constant falling and erection that ultimately shaped the Australian landscape.

Brolga

Long ago, when all had been made but was in total darkness, Brolga and Emu disputed as to the need for light in the world. Brolga said no, things were fine as they were. Emu said the animal people were forever bumping into each other and were unable to find their things when they had put them down. Brolga got very angry and clipped Emu's wings, making her a flightless bird. Emu avenged herself by tossing a brolga's egg into the sky. The egg exploded and became the sun. Now everybody can daily admire the beauty and colours of the great work of the Sky Father.

This story is virtually a replica of the stories found commonly among the Amerindians. In their tales, Emu is replaced by Grandmother Spider who, of all the animal people, was the only creature able to bring the gift of light into the world.

The Birth of the Sun

The sun was born of a brolga's egg which exploded after Emu tossed it into the sky, and from this explosion the rainbow also came into being. The rainbow is invariably associated with water which, because it falls from the sky and fertilizes Mother Earth, is both the seed and wisdom of Father Sky. The rainbow was termed pulwaiya (father's father), but it was both the divine phallus and the divine womb. As the essence of all life, it accompanied the aged Kunapipi when she went on her great walkabout.

Another story says that Punjel waited patiently for the Great Byamee to finish making everything; their home in the Milky Way was, in the meantime, extremely cold. Meanwhile, in anticipation of Byamee creating fire, Punjel built a very large woodpile. He then sat and amused himself by watching Emu and Eagle-Hawk scrapping over ownership of a carcass down on earth. Emu won the prize and an angry Eagle-Hawk tossed one of her eggs into the sky. It hit the huge woodpile, which then burst into flames and became the sun.

Mother Earth and Father Sky

In ancient nature religions, it is common to find the Goddess (earth spirit) in the form of a trinity or as triple-headed. In Aboriginal tradition, as previously mentioned, three women descended from the stars and two of them later returned; these are depicted here by the circles of dots. It is at the equinoxes (when the sun crosses the celestial equator) that Father Sky (the sun) and Mother Earth are joined as man and woman.

The task of separating these two passionate lovers was left to the magpies who, unable to use their wings, had tried walking around the cramped space between earth and sky. Thousands organised themselves and, with sticks in their beaks, they pushed against the sky in unison. Initially it was a very hard task, but it got easier as they made more and more space. Ultimately the sky split asunder and light flooded the world.

Yarandoo

It was a time when food was in short supply and many survived by catching and eating the rat kangaroo, but one man remembered the words of the great Byamee (he who brought the law from the All Father): 'The rat kangaroo is forbidden flesh.' So it was that this righteous man would sooner starve than break the law. In his wanderings he approached a tree, hoping he might find food there. A yowee spirit descended from it, picked up the man and took him into the tree, which uprooted itself and rose up to the heavens. It then manifested as the constellation called Yarandoo (the Southern Cross).

Rat kangaroos seem to be associated with star making, as is the mischievous bird Wahn, the crow who tricked Pewingi, the swamp hawk, into jumping on a bunch of echidna spines he had planted in a rat kangaroo's nest. But once they had grown into Pewingi's claws, this only helped him to better catch the rat kangaroo. Byamee ultimately put an end to his mischief by turning him into a star. The crows have never since ceased to laugh at Wahn's comeuppance—they greet each morning with Wah, Wah, Wah.

Crocodile Dreaming

This creature, wherever he appears, is a revered totem. He was a close companion of the Seven Sisters (in the Milky Way) when, as the result of a curse, they lived as water girls. But his real claim to fame is that each month, at full moon, he begins to tear strips from the moon man until he has completely devoured him. Whereupon, the moon man is reborn and the cycle begins again.

Bahloo, the moon, was also a victim of Wahn the crow. Bahloo lived in a cave way up in the side of a hill where he made girl babies and sent them down to married women in any quantity they required. Because he would not let Wahn make the boy babies, Wahn tricked him into climbing a tree for a feed of grubs. The trickster crow then uttered an incantation that made the tree grow up to the stars where Bahloo is now still stuck.

Goanna and Snake

These two creatures make frequent joint apperances in Aboriginal art. This is because, in her feminine aspect, Snake is an excavator of riverbeds and Goanna man was the inventor of the canoe. As an expert tree climber, he stripped the bark from a messmate tree and patiently sewed it into a boat which gave fishermen access to the deeper and more rewarding parts of the rivers.

Goannas were originally very industrious creatures who had arrived with the first migration from the thousand islands in the canoe belonging to Whale. But as they moved south through Australia, they gave up planting and reaping the vegetables they loved so much and took to preying upon small and defenceless creatures.

After childbirth, women were restricted to remaining by a fire; Snake, being a water spirit, would not molest them if they were close to the fire.

The Boomerang that Captured the Sun

Bila was the Sun Woman who daily sent out her dogs to capture victims, which she would cook on her fire and eat. On one momentous occasion, her dogs wiped out an entire tribe and brought the corpses to her as a gift. This incident was witnessed by Muda the gecko and Kudna the lizard, who decided it was time to bring an end to Bila's shenanigans. They set off on their journey to her camp, all the while swearing they would avenge the death of their friends. As they approached her she reached for a boomerang, but Kudna was faster than Bila and, when struck by his weapon, she turned into a fireball and vanished, leaving the world in darkness.

Fearful of the gloom and what they had done, these two fellows began throwing boomerangs to all points of the compass until one of them, thrown to the east, brought back the sun.

Kangaroo's Legs

When he first arrived in Australia on Whale's canoe, Kangaroo walked and ran just like any other four-legged creature, but he quickly found that men were eager to hunt him as a source of food. On one occasion, he spied a hunter approaching with spear in hand and took off into the bush, fully believing that his four legs would be faster than the man's two, but he was wrong and the chase persisted all day. It only ended when darkness fell. Kangaroo lay collapsed in an exhausted heap when he saw the hunter lighting a fire. 'I had better move quickly and quietly before the light exposes me,' said Kangaroo to himself. He raised himself on his hind legs to minimize the noise, and stealthily hopped away. Realising how easily he was moving, he decided that two legs—as with men—were obviously better than four. From that moment, his hind legs got stronger and his forepaws got shorter. That's why the kangaroo is as he is today.

Marmoo's Jealousy

Byamee had made the world and both he and it were at peace. Crystal-clear streams ran down from majestic mountains with peaks covered in snow. The great plains were covered with a lush green carpet and a multitude of flowers painted every imaginable colour. The only things that had not been made were the birds and insects. Meanwhile Marmoo, the Dark Spirit, looked down on this scene in jealousy and rage. 'I could have done better in less time,' he told his wife. Her simple response was: 'Show me.' 'I will,' he said, 'but first I must destroy Byamee's handiwork.'

In a cave where none could see, Marmoo created a vast horde of creeping, crawling, flying insects which, when he released them, proceeded to ravage the land and lay it to waste.

Byamee was desolate and came to see Nungeena, the spirit-woman he had left to supervise his creation. 'Don't worry, Father Byamee,' she said. 'I hid some flowers behind that waterfall.' Working with deft fingers, she quickly fashioned many birds from the flowers, and these flew off to feast upon the insects whose ravages the earth was able to quickly overcome.

How Death Came Into the World

The curlew men and women emerged from a crevice in a rock, but the women emerged first and this caused dissent and jealousy, which was aimed at the first man to appear. Ultimately the dissention turned to anger, the women separated from the men and the bone that brings death was pointed at this first man.

Racked with pain, he died and was buried in the stony soil. But on the following day the ground began to shake and he pushed head and shoulders out of his grave, all the while looking accusingly at the dumbstruck men around him. But Urbura the magpie raced to the rescue; he speared the undead man in the throat and stomped on him until he sank back into the ground. Urbura then flew off with the curlew women. Had the magpie not killed this man a second time, death would not have come into the world.

It isn't long before the visitor to Australia encounters the Aboriginal Dreamtime: a concept as unique, beautiful and mysterious as the land itself. And then there are the strange creatures, such as the kangaroo, duck-billed platypus, emu and goanna, who not only inhabit the land, but occupy the Dreamtime too, in the form of animal people.

So many travellers pass through this country unable to grasp even a little of the Dreaming knowledge. And that's a pity; it's a rich and exotic ocean for the soul to swim in. The object of this little book is to try to repair this to some degree.

Along with the politics of a new and caring attitude toward our much-beleaguered planet, there must come a spiritual overview—a new animism. This makes knowledge of the Australian Aboriginal Dreamtime imperative.

R Lewis

Drawing from an entire lifetime devoted to the study of ancient religion and myth, the author has provided a brief and concise insight into what is meant by the Dreamtime, followed by a unique collection of Dreamtime stories which will, undoubtedly, reach the little child in all of us.

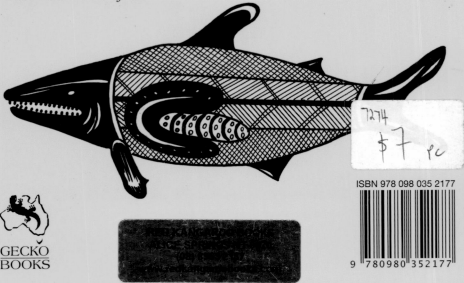

GECKO
BOOKS

ISBN 978 098 035 2177

9 780980 352177